The Baby Panda

by Jessica Quilty

illustrated by Nicole Wong

Target Skill Consonants Bb/b/ and Nn/n/
High-Frequency Words me, with, she

PEARSON

Scott
Foresman

Pam is at the zoo.

Tim is with Pam.

It is Bim.

Bim is with mom.

Bim is little like me.

Bim can nap.

Nap, Bim, nap.

Nap, nap, nap!

She can sit a bit.

Sit, Bim, sit.

Sit, sit, sit!

Bim can tap with me.

Tap, Bim, tap.

Tap, tap, tap!